S0-ADG-632

Building Grammar
Grades 3-4

By

Cynthia Salisbury

Cover Design by
Matthew Van Zomeren

Inside Illustrations by
Jill Wood

Published by Instructional Fair • TS Dension
an imprint of

McGraw-Hill
Children's Publishing

About the Author

Cynthia Salisbury is a teacher and writer with more than fifteen years of experience. She holds a bachelor's degree in liberal arts and language from California Lutheran University as well as a master's degree in multicultural education from Arizona State University, where she is enrolled in the creative writing program. Cynthia is a member of the Society of Children's Bookwriters and Illustrators and the Arizona Author's Association. She has also written Building Grammar for grades 1–2.

Credits

Author: Cynthia Salisbury
Illustrator: Jill wood
Project Director/Editor: Sara Bierling
Editors: Meredith Van Zomeren, Wendy Roh Jenks, Jane Haradine
Cover Design: Matthew Van Zomeren
Production: Tracy L. Wesorick

McGraw-Hill
Children's Publishing

A Division of The McGraw-Hill Companies

Published by Instructional Fair • TS Denison
An imprint of McGraw-Hill Children's Publishing
Copyright © 2001 McGraw-Hill Children's Publishing

Send all inquiries to:
McGraw-Hill Children's Publishing
3195 Wilson Drive NW
Grand Rapids, Michigan 49544

Building Grammar—grades 3–4
ISBN: 0-7424-0150-2

2 3 4 5 6 7 8 9 PHXBK 07 06 05 04 03 02

Table of Contents

Continental Flair

The **subject** of a sentence names who or what the sentence is about, and the **predicate** tells something about the subject or what the subject is doing.

<u>The old man</u> (paid for the newspaper.)

subject   predicate

Underline the subjects and circle the predicates in the following sentences.

1. Europe contains many countries.

2. Many people in Germany work in factories.

3. France produces many different cheeses.

4. Delicious chocolates are made in Switzerland.

5. Italy is famous for its pasta.

6. Russian ballet dancers are skillful.

7. Tulips are exported from the Netherlands.

8. The British like to drink tea.

9. Norwegians like to ski.

10. Many Spaniards enjoy attending bullfights.

An Island Adventure

The **subject** of a sentence tells who or what the sentence is about. The **predicate** of a sentence tells what the subject is or is doing.

The sailboat (took us to the island.)

    subject   predicate

In these sentences about a trip to an island, underline each subject and circle each predicate.

1. We all climbed aboard the boat for the trip to the island.

2. Aunt Betty took the tiller, and her sisters manned the sails.

3. The wind started to pick up as we pushed off from shore.

4. The lake was very quiet.

5. A few ducks followed our boat as we left.

6. I fed them crusts of bread from our sandwiches.

7. As we got closer to the island, I became more and more excited.

8. Aunt Betty gave me some binoculars to try to see the island.

9. Just as we got near the dock, I saw a man with a long beard wearing a strange dress.

10. Then I saw his house, which looked like a Chinese temple.

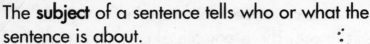

Up Periscope!

> The **subject** of a sentence tells who or what the sentence is about.
>
>   *The captain boarded the sub.*
>
> The **predicate** of a sentence tells what the subject is or what it does.
>
>   *The captain **boarded the sub**.*

Draw a line under the subject and circle the predicate of each sentence below.

1. The yellow submarine submerged under the ocean.

2. The captain yelled to the crew.

3. The navigator guided the sub to its first position.

4. On the way, they saw beautiful fish with bright colors.

5. The crew kept close watch once the sub arrived in the bay.

6. Crew members used binoculars to survey the land.

7. The killer whales had not appeared after four hours.

8. The captain decided to dock the submarine and wait until morning.

The Top of the Ocean

The **simple subject** of a sentence tells who or what the sentence is about and does not contain any adjectives or articles.

*The top of the **ocean** sometimes looks angry in a storm.*

The **complete subject** of a sentence is all the words in the part of the sentence that tells about the subject, including adjectives and articles.

***The top of the ocean** sometimes looks angry in a storm.*

Draw a line under the simple subject and circle the complete subject in the sentences below.

1. The killer whale is found in all oceans.

2. Killer whales, or orcas, travel in groups, or pods.

3. Pods can have from two to dozens of whales.

4. Each pod "talks" with its own set of underwater sounds.

5. Most of the crew members had seen orcas before.

6. The killer whale has teeth, unlike some other whales.

7. These whales feed on salmon and other fish.

8. They do not usually attack people.

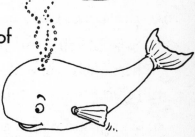

The Bottom of the Sea

The **simple predicate** of a sentence tells what the subject is or what the subject does and doesn't contain any modifying words, such as adverbs.

*He **takes** a trip to the bottom of the sea every year.*

The **complete predicate** of a sentence contains all the words in the action, or predicate, part of the sentence, including all modifiers.

*He **takes a trip to the bottom of the sea every year**.*

Underline the simple predicate and circle the complete predicate.

1. The crew decided to leave the ship and explore the ocean.

2. Some of the crew used snorkeling gear to explore near the surface of the water.

3. Others put on oxygen tanks so they could explore deeper under the water.

4. Each group had one hour to explore.

5. The snorkeling group had seen over 50 different kinds of fish by the time they returned to the sub.

6. The group with the oxygen tanks brought up something unusual with them.

7. The object was covered with barnacles and seaweed.

8. It was about the size of a suitcase.

Frog and Toad

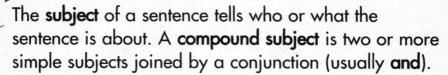

compound subject

> The **subject** of a sentence tells who or what the sentence is about. A **compound subject** is two or more simple subjects joined by a conjunction (usually **and**).
>
> ***Toads*** are amphibians.   ***Frogs*** are amphibians.
> ***Toads and frogs*** are amphibians.

If the sentence has a compound subject, write **CS** on the line. If the sentence does not have a compound subject, write **NO**.

 1. An amphibian lives in the water and on land.

 2. Frogs and salamanders are amphibians.

 3. A salamander has a long body and a tail.

 4. Adult frogs and toads do not have tails.

 5. It is easy for them to move on land.

 6. Frogs use their strong legs for leaping.

 7. Toads have shorter legs and cannot jump as far.

 8. The eyes and nose of a frog are on the top of its head.

 9. Tree frogs are expert jumpers and can cling to things.

 10. Toads and frogs cannot give people warts.

A Day at the Dentist

> The **predicate** of a sentence tells what the subject is or what the subject is doing. A **compound predicate** consists of two or more simple predicates joined by a conjunction (usually **and**).
>
> Dad *picks up* Troy.   Dad *takes* Troy to the dentist.
> Dad *picks up Troy and takes him* to the dentist.

If the sentence has a compound predicate, write **CP** on the line.
If the sentence does not have a compound predicate, write **NO**.

_____ 1. Dad and Troy park the car and go inside.

_____ 2. Troy reads and watches TV while waiting for the dentist.

_____ 3. Dad talks to another patient.

_____ 4. The hygienist comes into the room and gets Troy.

_____ 5. The hygienist cleans, polishes, and x-rays Troy's teeth.

_____ 6. The dentist examines Troy's teeth and checks the x-rays.

_____ 7. The dentist gives Troy a toothbrush to take home.

_____ 8. Troy thanks the dentist.

_____ 9. Dad pays the dentist.

_____ 10. Troy promises to brush his teeth twice daily.

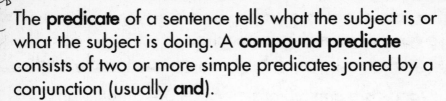

You're Out of Order!

> The words in a sentence must be in a certain **order** for the sentence to make sense.

Read the minutes of the Toon Town City Council meeting. The sentences are out of order. Write corrected sentences on the lines provided below.

1. Mayor Sneak called the order to meeting.

2. Was first on the agenda the escape of the circus animals.

3. Spoke about the escape Mrs. Greenshoes.

4. Suggested that all animals should be in cages an officer.

5. With Officer Bark all the members of the council agreed.

6. To the Gambezi Brothers the secretary wrote a letter.

1. _____

_____

2. _____

_____

3. _____

_____

4. _____

_____

5. _____

_____

6. _____

The Circus Clowns

When two or more **simple sentences** are joined together, they become a **compound sentence.** The conjunctions that may be used to join sentences are **and**, **but**, and **or**. Remember to place a comma before the conjunction.

Mayor Sneak hired a circus.
The circus came to town with clowns and animals.

Mayor Sneak hired a circus, **and** *it came to town with clowns and animals.*

See if you can combine these sentences about clowns using a comma and a conjunction. Write the new sentence on the line.

1. Lanky Hank is as tall as the elephants. Stubby Sybill is as short as her miniature pony.

   _____

   _____

2. Princess Priscilla always wears a party hat. Prince Paulo wears a beanie.

   _____

   _____

3. Fire Hydrant Hank rides a tiny fire engine. His dalmatian rides with him.

   _____

   _____

Prickly Plants

A **sentence fragment** is only a part of a sentence. It does not express a complete thought.

fragment: *After tomorrow, if I pass the test.*
sentence: *After tomorrow, if I pass the test, I will graduate.*

Write an **S** on the line before the sentences that are complete. Write an **F** on the line before the sentences that are fragments.

S 1. The pincushion cactus looks just like Mom's pincushion for sewing.

F 2. Prickly pear cactus and hedgehog cactus.

F 3. Sucks up water when it rains.

S 4. Spines help.

S 5. The agave and ocotillo thrive in the desert.

These sentences are missing something. Finish them by drawing a line to the parts that match.

a. All cactuses

b. do not need a lot of water to live.

c. Cactus flowers

d. can't eat cactuses because of the spines.

e. The stem of the cactus

f. Cactuses

g. can be white, yellow, red, or orange.

h. Animals

i. stores water for dry spells.

j. have roots close to the top of the sand.

Who's the Stranger?

Declarative sentences make statements or tell something. They begin with capital letters and end with periods.

I saw a stranger in Toon Town.

Interrogative sentences ask questions. They begin with capital letters and end with question marks.

Who is the stranger?

Read all the telling and asking sentences that Farley Facts wrote down after his interview. Put an **I** (interrogative sentence) by the questions and a **D** (declarative sentence) by the statements. Then add the correct punctuation to each sentence.

Farley Facts: _____ Are you a stranger to Toon Town

Stranger: _____ I am new to your fine city

_____ Toon Town is a beautiful place

Farley Facts: _____ Why did you come to Toon Town

Stranger: _____ I have a special job to do

Farley Facts: _____ What is your job

Stranger: _____ It is top secret

_____ I am part of a team

_____ We will be digging in the dirt

Farley Facts: _____ Is there anything else you can tell us

Stranger: _____ Yes, I am a doctor

_____ I study bones

The Crafty Critter

Imperative sentences command or make a request. The subject of these sentences is usually "**you**," although it is usually not stated. A command starts with a capital letter and ends with a period.

Get the critter before it escapes.

Exclamations are used to show strong feelings, such as anger or surprise. They begin with a capital letter and end with an exclamation mark (!).

Ouch! It bit me!

See if you can sort out this 911 phone conversation with Mrs. Greenshoes. Underline the commands. Put a star next to the exclamations.

1. "Tell me what kind of critters you see, Mrs. Greenshoes."

2. "They have big teeth! I'm scared!"

3. "Close your windows and doors."

4. "Oh, no! They're on my porch!"

5. "Lock your door, Mrs. Greenshoes. Officer Leash is on his way."

6. "I locked the door. I need help fast!"

7. "Officer Leash's white truck should be there any minute. Wave to him so he knows where you are."

8. "Okay. The beast just ate my petunias!"

The Grand Canyon

Ending punctuation marks help a reader know when a thought stops. A **period** is used at the end of a **declarative** or **imperative** sentence. An **exclamation mark** is used at the end of an **exclamatory** sentence. A **question mark** is used at the end of an **interrogative** sentence.

Read the following paragraphs about the Grand Canyon. Add ending punctuation to make the sentences clear.

The Grand Canyon has many trails   These trails were made by deer, sheep, and the native people of the region   When the sun sets, the canyon changes color   How many colors can you see   It is very scary to look over the edge   The view is beautiful

On the canyon wall, we saw some Native-American paintings   The designs on the rocks are called pictographs   They are symbols of objects from long ago   Have you ever seen pictographs

We saw people running the river   Do you know what running the river is   Climb aboard   It's a chance to ride the Colorado River on a raft   Wow You'll get the ride of your life

The Big Top

A **period** is used at the end of a **declarative** or **imper-ative** sentence. A **question mark** is used at the end of an **interrogative** sentence. An **exclamation point** is used at the end of an **exclamatory** sentence.

The clown entertained the audience.
What time will the performance start?
Oh, no, there's a lion!
Watch out for the ferocious lion.

Write the correct punctuation at the end of each sentence.
Write what kind of sentence it is in the blank: **declarative (D)**, **imperative (IM)**, **interrogative (IN)**, or **exclamatory (E)**.

__D__ 1. The circus had its beginnings in ancient Rome.

__D__ 2. The modern circus developed in England and soon came to America.

__IN__ 3. Did Barnum and Bailey and the Ringling Brothers combine their two circuses?

__D__ 4. Their circus became the biggest and most famous in history.

__E__ 5. Watch out for the tigers!

__Im__ 6. Watch the performers fly through the air from one trapeze to another.

__E__ 7. What an exciting place the "big top" is for everyone!

__Im__ 8. Look at the lion tamer cracking his whip.

Weird Water Creatures

A **declarative** sentence can easily be changed to an **interrogative** sentence.

The dinosaur exhibit is one of the best.
Is the dinosaur exhibit one of the best?

Read the sentences below. Change each one from a statement to a question and write it on the line.

1. The crew took underwater pictures of fish.

   _____

   _____

2. Some fish glowed in the dark like neon.

   _____

   _____

3. Other fish glided through the water like birds through the air.

   _____

   _____

4. None of the crew members knew the names of the fish they found.

   _____

   _____

5. Someone found a book in the ship's library that described most of the fish they had seen.

   _____

   _____

Noun Hunt

A **noun** is a word that names a person, place, or thing.

Fill in each blank with a noun that makes sense.

1. My _____ was barking.

2. _____ is extremely cold.

3. A _____ has many colors.

4. The red _____ is pretty.

5. The living room _____ is on.

6. John rode the _____ to school.

7. Sally read her favorite _____.

8. She had a _____ on her face.

9. I sat in a comfortable _____.

10. I play the _____ well.

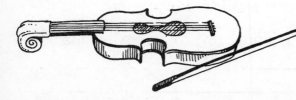

The Big Parade

> Some nouns are used to represent groups. These are called **collective nouns** and are used with a singular verb.
>
> The **mob** of children was excited for the parade to start.

First, underline the main collective noun in each sentence. Then, circle the singular verb that goes with each collective noun.

1. The crowd of people (was, were) scared by Aunt Betty's backfiring Model T.

2. The army (wear, wears) blue uniforms in the parade.

3. The Boy Scout troop (throw, throws) candy to the children.

4. The football team (marches, march) behind the Boy Scouts.

5. The largest group in the parade (is, are) the high school marching band.

6. The parade committee (ride, rides) on a float covered with yellow daisies.

7. The public (follows, follow) the last float to Scholarly Boulevard.

8. The school (has, have) a picnic for everyone.

9. The school choir (sing, sings) several songs for the people.

On Vacation

A **proper noun** names a specific person, place, or thing and is always capitalized.

John went to *St. Louis* to visit the *Gateway Arch*.

Circle the proper nouns in each sentence.

1. The students in Mr. Green's class at Elton Elementary visited many places during their summer vacations.

2. In June, Tanya visited her sister, Becky, in Georgia.

3. When she was in Atlanta, she saw a baseball game at Fulton County Stadium.

4. Tremel had fun at Universal Studios in Orlando, Florida.

5. His family also went to the Kennedy Space Center.

6. Carla enjoyed a ride on the Powell Street cable car in San Francisco.

7. Then she took a boat ride to Alcatraz and saw the Golden Gate Bridge.

8. Last Thursday, Carmen brought her pictures of Niagara Falls to show us.

9. She said she had a better time than when she saw the Royal Gorge in Colorado.

That's a Grand Canyon!

Proper nouns name specific people, places, or things and always begin with a capital letter.

*Today, my friend **Sara** and I are going to the **Grand Canyon** in **Arizona**.*

Look at the words in the lists below. Capitalize the beginning of each proper noun.

lizard	tarantula
deer	rattlesnake
point imperial	arizona
grand canyon	native american
phantom ranch	havasu canyon
kaibab trail	cactus
sheep	beaver
colorado river	rampart cave

Nature Hike

A **singular noun** names one person, place, or thing.

*The **class** went on a **field trip** to the **forest**.*

A **plural noun** names more than one person, place, or thing.

*The **classes** went on **field trips** to the **forests**.*

Underline the singular nouns with one line and the plural nouns with two lines.

1. One girl saw three deer run across the field.

2. Squirrels were running up and down the sides of the trees.

3. A bunny scurried under a bush.

4. As the children watched, some Canada geese flew overhead.

5. Pictures in books helped the children to identify many animals.

Write a sentence for each of these singular or plural nouns.

(berries) _____

(tree) _____

(man) _____

(women) _____

At the Game

> A **plural noun** names more than one person, place, or thing. Add **s** to make most nouns plural.
>
> *boys, parks, baseballs*
>
> If a noun ends in **sh**, **ch**, **x**, **s**, or **ss**, add **es** to form the plural.
>
> *wish**es**, lunch**es**, box**es**, gas**es**, glass**es***

Make each noun in parentheses plural by adding **s** or **es**. Write the plural nouns in the blanks.

All the _____ and _____ sat on
　　　　　　(mother)　　　　　　　　　(father)

_____ to watch the _____. The
　(bench)　　　　　　　　　　　　(game)

_____ ran onto the field to the _____
　(team)　　　　　　　　　　　　　　　　　(cheer)

of the crowd. In the first game, Alyce got two _____
　　　　　　　　　　　　　　　　　　　　　　　　(hit)

and no _____. Manuel made three fine
　　　　(strike)

_____ for his _____. The two
　(catch)　　　　　　　(teammate)

_____ were proud of the _____.
　(coach)　　　　　　　　　　　　　　(kid)

More and More

Follow these rules to form some plural nouns.

If a singular noun ends in a **vowel** and a **y**, add an **s**.

   day = days   *toy = toys*

If a singular noun ends in a **consonant** and a **y**, change the **y** to an **i** and add **es**.

   fly = flies   *candy = candies*

If a singular noun ends in **f** or **fe**, change the **f** or **fe** to a **v** and add **es**.

   thief = thieves   *life = lives*

Write the plural form of each noun.

1. baby _____
2. turkey _____
3. knife _____
4. sky _____
5. pansy _____
6. guppy _____
7. elf _____
8. wife _____
9. try _____

10. key _____
11. boy _____
12. shelf _____
13. lady _____
14. chimney _____
15. hoof _____
16. gypsy _____
17. monkey _____
18. lobby _____

Fiesta Fun!

> **Plural nouns** name more than one person, place, or thing.

Write the correct plural for each underlined noun on the line.

_____ 1. The lady at the stove was making <u>tortilla</u>.

_____ 2. The dessert on the menu had <u>peach</u> and custard.

_____ 3. The shelves in the restaurant held piñatas and colorful <u>box</u>.

_____ 4. The piñatas were filled with <u>candy</u> wrapped in colorful papers.

_____ 5. The women and the <u>girl</u> were dressed in colorful skirts.

_____ 6. The <u>man</u> and the children danced around a huge sombrero.

_____ 7. There were several <u>family</u> at the fiesta with lots of boys.

_____ 8. The fiesta was on the patio where a tree dropped <u>leaf</u> in the wind.

_____ 9. For dinner we had plates of <u>bean</u>, rice, and tamales.

In the Woods

> **Object pronouns** are used in the predicate of a sentence to take the place of the person, place, or thing that is the object of the sentence. Object pronouns include **me**, **you**, **her**, **him**, **it**, **us**, and **them**.
>
> *He wanted to find **a dinosaur**.*
> *He wanted to find **it**.*

Replace the objects in these sentences with the correct object pronouns.

1. Henry took the duty of standing guard, then he turned it over to <u>Maya</u>. _____

2. Everyone wanted to thank <u>Chuck</u> for making the dinner.

   _____

3. After we washed the dishes, we gathered around the fire to listen to <u>Hillary</u> sing. _____

4. We were just about ready for bed when we heard <u>a strange noise</u>. _____

5. Several crew members raced to the river and saw <u>a large, furry shape</u>. _____

6. But the mysterious visitor was too quick for most of <u>the crew</u>. _____

7. Javier ran after <u>the mysterious creature</u>.

   _____

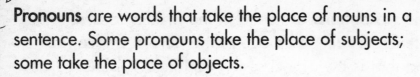

Surfers and Sailors

Pronouns are words that take the place of nouns in a sentence. Some pronouns take the place of subjects; some take the place of objects.

subject pronouns: I, you, he, she, it, we, they
object pronouns: me, you, him, her, it, us, them

Write the correct pronoun (subject or object) above each word to replace the underlined noun.

1. As <u>the *Nautilus*</u> cruised along the shore, <u>the crew</u> could see <u>surfers</u> riding huge waves.

2. When <u>the submarine</u> docked, <u>hundreds of sailors</u> were on the wharf to greet the ship.

3. After <u>everyone</u> had left <u>the ship</u>, <u>the captain</u> received orders for another assignment.

4. <u>The message</u> asked that <u>the crew</u> and <u>the submarine</u> be ready to depart for Mexico.

5. <u>The captain</u> knew where <u>the *Nautilus*</u> was going next.

6. The trip had something to do with <u>whales</u>.

7. There are a lot of <u>whales</u> in the Gulf region because <u>the water</u> is warmer there.

I, Me, We, Us

> **I** and **we** are subject pronouns. **Me** and **us** are object pronouns.
>
> *Mark and **I** are on our way to the park.*
> *Please feel welcome to join **us**.*

Choose the correct pronoun in the parentheses for each sentence. Write it in the blank.

1. _____ plan to launch rockets in the park on Saturday.
   (we, us)

2. Joel bought _____ a two-stage rocket.
   (I, me)

3. Kate and _____ both brought fresh batteries for
   (I, me)
   the launcher.

4. Manuel plans to build _____ a rocket.
   (we, us)

5. Officer Bark wants _____ to attend the rocket
   safety course.   (I, me)

6. _____ always paint the fins hot pink.
   (I, me)

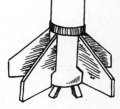

Penguins

A **pronoun** is a word that takes the place of a noun.

Meg gave the ball to Dave.
***He** was glad to get **it**.*

Read the sentences below. In the blank after each pronoun, write the word or words for which the pronoun stands.

Most penguins live near the South Pole. They (___They___) spend most of their time underwater searching for food. Penguins surface for air and get enough of it (_____) to fill the air sacs throughout their bodies. These (_____) make it possible for them (_____) to stay underwater for long periods of time.

Penguins feel best in very cold water but leave it (_____) to nest and raise their young. A penguin's nest is very odd. It (_____) is simply a pile of stones on a rocky shore. The female lays from one to three eggs. They (_____) are chalky white. After a time, the female passes her eggs on to the male. He (_____) tucks them (_____) under a skin flap on his body to keep them (_____) warm. It (_____) is lined with thick, soft down. The parents take turns feeding the babies when they (_____) hatch.

At first, the babies are covered with down. Later, they (_____) grow feathers on their bodies and scaly feathers on their wings. Before long, they (_____) go to sea with the adults to catch fish.

Island Expedition

Some words can be either **nouns** or **verbs**, depending on how they are used in a sentence.

*noun: The **paint** on Aunt Betty's shutters is wet.*
*verb: They will **paint** the shutters again later today.*

Decide if the word in bold type is used as a noun or a verb. Write **N** for noun or **V** for verb on the line before each sentence.

V 1. We will **ship** the picnic basket to the island.

N 2. Aunt Betty said we need to look for a **ship**.

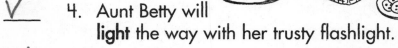

N 3. There will be hardly any **light** in the forest.

V 4. Aunt Betty will **light** the way with her trusty flashlight.

N 5. We parked our car near the **water**.

V 6. On the way, Aunt Betty stopped to **water** some flowers.

N 7. Then she picked some of the pink ones and put them in a **box**.

V 8. "I will **box** these for my friend in Hawaii," Aunt Betty said.

N 9. "It will be a **present** for my friend."

V 10. "I hope to **present** it to her tomorrow."

Heigh Ho! Heigh Ho!

> **Action verbs** show some kind of action. They are used to show what someone or something does, did, or will do.
>
> We **hike** down the trail.

Underline the action verbs in each hiking rule.

Hiking Rules

1. Everyone should walk, not run, on the trails.

2. Please throw away trash.

3. Do not drop or throw rocks into the canyon.

4. When you hike down to the bottom, you may camp only in the campground.

5. Build fires only in marked areas.

6. Store your food in a nearby tree.

7. Stop to let faster hikers pass you.

8. On hot days, take plenty of water and wear a hat.

Seedlings

The subject and verb in a sentence must agree in number.

*An adult **plant makes** seeds.*
*Adult **plants make** seeds.*

If the subject and verb agree, circle the **Yes** in front of each sentence. If they do not agree, circle the **No.**

(Yes) No   1. Seeds travel in many ways.

Yes (No)   2. Sometimes seeds falls into the water.

Yes (No)   3. They may floats a long distance.

(Yes) No   4. Animals gather seeds in the fall.

Yes (No)   5. Squirrels digs holes to bury their seeds.

Yes (No)   6. Cardinals likes to eat sunflower seeds.

(Yes) No   7. The wind scatters seeds, too.

Yes (No)   8. Dogs carries seeds that are stuck in their fur.

(Yes) No   9. Some seeds stick to people's clothing.

(Yes) No   10. People plant seeds to grow baby plants, called seedlings.

Welcome Tall Walls
subject-verb agreement

> The subject and verb in a sentence must agree in number.
>
> **One** of my friends **is** going to see the Grand Canyon.

Read about the student visitors in Arizona. Use the past tense to make the subjects and verbs agree. Be careful! One verb should be in the present tense.

1. Thirty-five students _____ on their way to the Grand
   (to be)

   Canyon.

2. One of the students _____ a fear of heights and
   (to have)

   _____ afraid to hike down the narrow trails.
   (to be)

3. "There _____ one more stop before we get to the
   (to be)

   canyon," the bus driver said as he stopped the big bus.

4. When he stopped, there _____ thirty-five students
   (to be)

   who got off the bus and _____ to see the sands of
   (to go)

   the Painted Desert.

Yesterday or Today

present and past tense

> Verbs that show action happening now are in the **present** tense. Verbs that show action happening in the past are in the **past** tense.
>
> **present**: *The man runs down the street.*
> **past**: *The man ran away.*

Circle the verb (present or past) that completes the action in the following sentences.

1. The Police Department (chases, chased) criminals every day.

2. Two days ago, our team (won, wins) the town trophy.

3. My teacher always (wears, wore) glasses.

4. The mailman (delivers, delivered) the wrong mail yesterday.

5. At last night's game, the mayor's daughter (sing, sang) the "Star Spangled Banner."

6. A fire truck (races, raced) down the street this morning.

7. The bank (opens, opened) at 8 a.m. on Mondays.

8. When the score was (tie, tied), the pitcher walked the winning run home.

9. I (worked, work) at the library last week.

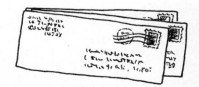

In the Past

When a verb tells something about the past, it is in the **past tense**. You can change most verbs to the past tense by adding **ed** or **d** to the basic form.

walk = walked   *bake = baked*

When the verb ends in a **y** after a consonant, change the **y** to an **i** and add **ed**.

hurry = hurried   *try = tried*

When the verb ends in a single consonant after a single short vowel, double the final consonant, then add **ed**.

stop = stopped   *knit = knitted*

Change each of the following verbs to the past tense.

1. study _____

2. bake _____

3. smell _____

4. wash _____

5. smile _____

6. grab _____

7. copy _____

8. trim _____

9. name _____

10. spy _____

11. melt _____

12. clip _____

13. toast _____

14. pop _____

15. empty _____

16. play _____

Who Are the Explorers?

Some verbs do not add **ed** to change to the past tense. They are called **irregular verbs**.

flew, sang, ran, swam, began, ate

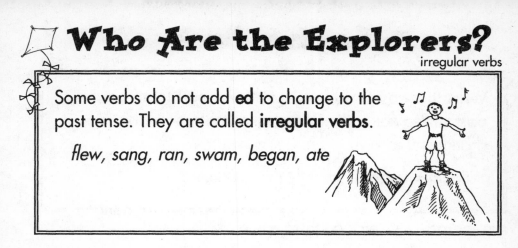

The digging crew took two days off from work to rest. Read what each crew member did. Underline all the irregular verbs.

1. Jeremy climbed to the top of the mountain and sang.

2. Moisha ran from our tent through town and back.

3. After breakfast on Tuesday, Tony and Cara went into town and bought books.

4. Jennifer found a stable, rented a horse, and rode on a trail by the river.

5. I put on my bathing suit and swam in the Rio Salado.

6. Dr. Dexterous flew a helicopter over the site and found the place where we should start our new dig.

7. Yolanda went exploring and found an arrowhead.

8. Carl found the best Mexican restaurant and ate tacos and tortilla chips.

To the Park

Verbs that do not add **ed** to form the past tense are called **irregular verbs**. The spelling of these verbs changes.

begin = began   *eat = ate*

Write the past tense of each irregular verb below.

1. Sam almost _____ (fall) when he tripped over the curb.

2. Diana made sure she _____ (take) bug spray on her hike.

3. Dave _____ (run) over to his friend's house.

4. Tim _____ (break) off a long piece of grass to put in his mouth.

5. Eve _____ (know) the path along the river well.

6. The clouds _____ (begin) to turn gray.

7. Kathy _____ (throw) a small piece of bread to the ducks.

8. Everyone _____ (eat) a very nutritious meal after the long adventure.

9. We all _____ (sleep) very well that night.

A Morning Stroll

Past tense verbs that are not formed by adding **ed** or **d** are called **irregular verbs**.

present	past	past participle
ring	rang	(has, have) rung
see	saw	(has, have) seen

Fill in the missing verbs in the chart.

Present	Past	Past Participle
do, does		(has or have) done
go, goes	went	(has or have)
know, knows		(has or have) known
fall, falls		(has or have) fallen
speak, speaks	spoke	(has or have)
stand, stands		(has or have) stood
write, writes		(has or have) written
draw, draws	drew	(has or have)

Circle the correct past tense verb in the parentheses.

1. Dad and I (went, gone) on a walk in the park one morning.

2. More than six inches of snow had (fall, fallen).

3. The tall trees (stand, stood) silently in their white overcoats.

4. A rabbit (ran, run) away as we approached.

5. We (heard, hears) a cardinal's call from the oak tree.

6. A squirrel (sat, sitted) in a tree overhead.

7. It (took, taken) us nearly an hour to return home.

Aunt Betty's List

Verb tense tells time in a sentence. The **future tense** tells about what will happen at a later time. **Will** is usually used with the verb to show future time.

*Tomorrow we **will go** to Kathmandu.*

Here is a list that Aunt Betty had on her refrigerator. Fix the list by writing each sentence in the future tense.

1. This afternoon I pick up groceries at the store.

   _____

   _____

2. I call the painter to paint the shutters.

   _____

   _____

3. The neighborhood builds a float for the parade next Friday.

   _____

   _____

4. The picnic lunch at City Hall is tomorrow.

   _____

   _____

5. Jenny comes on Thursday.

   _____

   _____

The Big Helper

A **helping verb** is used with another verb to "help" it show action.

*I **was** turning.*
*He **should have** turned.*
*They **must have been** turning.*

Complete the sentences below by filling in a verb phrase that uses the verb shown and a helping verb from the Word Bank below.

1. The flowers ___are growing___ tall.
   (to grow)

2. Freddie ___Should listen___ in class.
   (to listen)

3. Lori ___has to eat___ her vegetables.
   (to eat)

4. I ___Will do___ my homework later.
   (to do)

5. They ___might go___ to the movie.
   (to go)

Word Bank

could	would	does	been	are
can	should	~~do~~	being	am
must	~~will~~	had	be	is
~~might~~	shall	have	were	was
may	did	has		

Have You?

A **verb** may be a single word or a group of words. A verb with more than one word is made of a **main verb** and one or more **helping verbs**.

*Mike **can** usually **win** at Scrabble.*

helping   main

In the following sentences, underline the main verb and circle the helping verb(s).

1. Have you seen my new car?

2. Carlos did not tell anyone his secret.

3. I am usually working on Saturdays.

4. Deb has gone to the meeting at school.

5. She is swimming in the lake.

6. You should never chew gum in class.

7. Fran cannot get her locker open.

8. Did your older sister marry Tim?

9. I have been to my violin lesson.

10. I might not finish this large pizza.

11. I have never been to Hawaii.

Fire!

A **verb phrase** contains a **main verb** and a **helping verb**. **Has** and **have** can be used as helping verbs.

*We **have learned** about firefighting.*

Underline the helping verb and circle the main verb in each sentence.

1. A firefighter has come to talk to our class.

2. We have written questions to ask her.

3. I have wondered how you become a firefighter.

4. We have waited to be shown the firefighter's uniform.

5. We have learned about home fire safety.

6. We have planned escape routes from our homes.

7. I have made an escape plan so that my entire family will be safe.

8. Most of us have known the dangers of matches for a long time.

9. The teacher has given us a list of items that easily catch on fire.

10. Many students have seen these things in their homes.

Sippin' Sarsaparilla

A **linking verb** connects the subject of a sentence to the words in the predicate. Forms of the verb **to be** (*is, are, am*) are the most frequently used linking verbs.

I **am** sick.
Mrs. Potter **is** our neighbor.

Use the linking verbs below to fill in the cactus captions.

> ## Linking Verbs
>
> is   am   was   are   were

1. The oldest saguaro _____ over 250 years old.

2. The cactus wrens _____ in the hole.

3. The coyotes _____ wild.

4. I _____ cold as I paddle down the river.

5. The saguaro _____ a flowering plant.

6. The flower of the saguaro _____ the state flower of Arizona.

Our Forefathers

> A **linking verb** does not show action. It links the subject of a sentence with a noun or adjective in the predicate. Forms of **to be** can be linking verbs.
>
> *Thomas Jefferson **was** a president of the United States.*

Write a linking verb in each blank.

1. The class writing assignment ___is___ a report on U.S. Presidents.

2. The due date for our report ___is___ tomorrow.

3. I ___am___ glad I chose to write about Thomas Jefferson.

4. He ___was___ the youngest delegate to the First Continental Congress.

5. The colonies ___were___ angry at England.

6. Thomas Jefferson ___was___ a great writer, so he was asked to help write the Declaration of Independence.

7. The signing of that document ___was___ an important historical event.

8. As President, Jefferson ___was___ responsible for organizing the Louisiana Purchase.

9. He ___was___ the second president to live in the White House.

10. Americans ___are___ fortunate for the part Thomas Jefferson played in our country's history.

Is It Helping or Not?

Forms of the verb **to be** can be used as **main verbs** or **helping verbs**.

*main: They **are** quiet.*

*helping: They **are being** quiet.*

Circle the form of **to be** in each sentence below. Then write **main** or **helping** on the line to the left of each sentence to show how the verb is being used.

_____1. Ruth has been playing soccer every day this week.

_____2. He was teaching us to read.

_____3. The lunches were disgusting.

_____4. Janie was planning on skipping school.

_____5. My baby sister is stubborn.

Circle the correct form of *to be* in the parentheses. Then rewrite the sentence.

1. Julie (been, has been) the best student in our class.

_____

2. Manuel (be, will be) a very good scientist.

_____

3. Soon, he (been, will be) a student hall monitor.

_____

Sports Do's

> It is important to use the correct form of the verb **to do** whenever you speak or write.
>
> *Tara and Nan **do** stretching exercises.*
> *Sara **did** the most laps.*

Circle the correct form of *to do* in each sentence.

1. Our soccer team (did, done) a great job last year.

2. They have (did, done) very well this year.

3. John (do, does) thirty sit-ups every morning.

4. Tara and Nan (do, does) laps in the afternoon.

5. Sara (do, does) the most practicing each day.

6. Our team (does, do) have a lot of spirit.

7. We (doesn't, don't) ever get tired.

8. Mary (doesn't, don't) always stop the ball.

9. Our coach (did, do) compliment us for our efforts.

10. Playing soccer well (do, does) require long hours of practice.

Pretty Petals

Adjectives answer **which one, how many,** or **what kind.**
These three red apples.

Circle the adjectives in the sentences below. Then write the adjectives you circled under the correct category for each sentence.

1. Those lovely pink carnations each have five blossoms.

2. These white roses have a sweet fragrance.

3. Each flower has several dainty petals.

4. The refreshing aroma of the sweet-scented lavender filled the air.

5. These five colorful canna are tall plants.

Which one?	What kind?	How many?
1. _____	_____	_____
2. _____	_____	_____
3. _____	_____	_____
4. _____	_____	_____
5. _____	_____	_____

Sunnier or Cloudiest?

> Add **er** to most **adjectives** when comparing two nouns. Add **est** to most adjectives when comparing three or more nouns.
>
> *The forecaster said this winter is **colder** than last winter.*
> *It is the **coldest** winter on record.*

Write the correct comparative form of the adjective on the line.

1. The weather map showed that the _____ place of all was Marquette, Michigan. (cold)

2. The _____ city was Phoenix, Arizona. (warm)

3. Does San Diego get _____ than San Francisco? (hot)

4. The _____ snow fell in the Twin Cities. (deep)

5. The snowfall was two inches _____ than in Buffalo. (deep)

6. The _____ place was Chicago, Illinois. (windy)

7. The _____ winds blew there. (strong)

8. The _____ city in the U.S. was Bangor, Maine. (foggy)

9. Seattle was the _____ the city. (rainy)

An Exciting Day

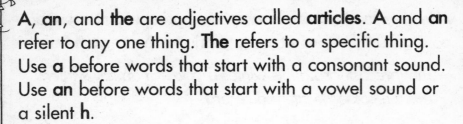

A, **an**, and **the** are adjectives called **articles**. A and **an** refer to any one thing. **The** refers to a specific thing. Use **a** before words that start with a consonant sound. Use **an** before words that start with a vowel sound or a silent **h**.

*Every duck in **the** pond wanted **a** bath.*
*It was **an** easy thing to do in **an** hour.*

Complete the story below by filling in the articles **a**, **an**, or **the**.

_____ park on Saturday was full of animals. _____ ant was nibbling on my sandwich before I could get it in my mouth! _____ deer was behind _____ fence watching all _____ animals and people. _____ children were running and leaping through _____ grass, chasing _____ chipmunk. _____ park ranger made sure _____ picnic area was kept clean. When I looked down by my feet, I spotted _____ apple slice there. It wasn't there for long, though. Before I could pick it up, _____ squirrel snatched it and ran away! _____ sun was peeking through _____ thick-leaved trees and casting just enough warmth for _____ turtle that was wading in _____ pond. Even though I was only at _____ park for _____ hour, it was my most exciting visit ever.

Venting Volcanoes

An **adverb** tells more about a verb. Adverbs can tell how, when, or where an action takes place.

how: Kallie drove the car **slowly**.
when: Kallie drove the car **then**.
where: Kallie drove the car **far**.

Read about the volcanoes and underline the adverbs that tell how, when, or where something happened.

Tuesday, April 22

Washington State

Our pilot landed carefully in a valley near Mount Saint Helens. As we left the safety of the helicopter, we all looked up the valley to see the dome of the volcano. It looked far away, and it seemed long ago that it had erupted. The volcano destroyed many forests, cities, and farms. The violent eruption in 1980 happened quickly. Tragically, 57 people died.

Friday, April 25

Oregon

Mount Shasta stands quietly within its blanket of snow. It is one of the highest mountains in the Cascade Mountain Range. Only Mount Rainier is taller. As we hiked slowly toward the peak, we could still see some signs of its many eruptions. We could see where the magma had erupted quietly and flowed slowly from the vent.

Ten Terrific Tips

> An **adverb** tells more about a verb. Adverbs can tell when, where, or how an action takes place.
>
> *I sleep **often**.*

See if you can find the correct adverb in the Word Bank to finish these ten terrific tips about hiking.

1. When hiking in the desert, _____ stay on the marked trails.

2. Don't go too _____ a rattlesnake, or it will attack.

3. Stay _____ away from washes during storms; the water can be dangerous.

4. Apply sunscreen _____.

5. Take breaks _____; don't wear yourself out.

6. When walking in the desert, walk _____ and _____.

7. Approach any strange object _____.

Word Bank

near	slowly	always	frequently
far	carefully	generously	cautiously

   IF0371 *Building Grammar*

Let's Go!

> **Adverbs** show comparison by adding **er** or **est** to the end of the word. Add **er** when using an adverb to compare two actions. Add **est** when using an adverb to compare three or more actions. Add more, most, less, or least to adverbs ending in *ly*.
>
> *The clarinets played **more loudly** than the flutes.*
> *The trumpets played **most loudly** of all the instruments.*

Finish the following sentences by using a comparative form of the underlined adverb.

1. The airplane flew <u>high</u>.
   The airplane flew _____ than the bird.
   The jet flew _____ of all.

2. Jack's car raced <u>fast</u>.
   Jim's car raced _____ than Jack's.
   Ted's car raced _____ of all.

Add *more*, *most*, *less*, or *least* to each adverb to show comparison.

1. Andrew travels overseas _____ frequently than Eric

2. Vanessa travels overseas _____ frequently of all her friends.

3. Raquel drives her car _____ skillfully than Sara.

4. Dave drives _____ expertly.

5. Aaron uses his boat _____ frequently than Tim.

The Right Stuff

Sometimes people have difficulty using **good**, **well**, **sure**, **surely**, **real**, and **really** correctly. This chart may help you.

Adjectives	Adverbs
Good is an adjective when it describes a noun. *That was a **good** dinner.*	**Good** is never used as an adverb.
Well is an adjective when it means in good health or having a good appearance. *She looks **well**.*	**Well** is an adverb when it is used to tell that something is done capably or effectively. *She writes **well**.*
Sure is an adjective when it modifies a noun. *A robin is a **sure** sign of spring.*	**Surely** is an adverb. *He **surely** wants a job.*
Real is an adjective that means genuine or true. *That was a **real** diamond.*	**Really** is an adverb. *Mary **really** played a good game.*

Use the chart to help you write the correct word in each blank.

1. You did a very _____ job cleaning your room.
2. The detective in the story used his skills _____.
3. Len _____ wanted to finish before everyone else.
4. I _____ want to read that book now.
5. Did it take long to decide who the _____ criminal was?
6. The class hamster looked _____ and healthy.
7. Kwan read _____ as she worked on the story problem.
8. You will _____ get a good grade on that report.

Three Cheers!

A **possessive noun** shows ownership or possession. Add an **apostrophe** and an **s** to a singular noun. Add an **apostrophe** and an **s** to a plural noun that does not end in **s**. Add an **apostrophe** to a plural noun that ends in **s** or **es**.

the **dog's** bone
the **children's** turtle
the **babies'** playpen

Read the sentences. Circle the answers that show how many people possess something.

1. Our class's talent show was last Friday.
   How many classes had a talent show? **one** **more than one**

2. The students' talents were interesting.
   How many students had talents? **one** **more than one**

3. The girl's baton flew in the air.
   How many girls had a baton? **one** **more than one**

4. Jacob's talent was yodeling.
   How many students can yodel? **one** **more than one**

5. The ballet dancers' act was after the musician's.
   How many ballet dancers were there? **one** **more than one**

6. The students' cheering was loud.
   How many students cheered? **one** **more than one**

7. The principal's clapping was noisy.
   How many principals were clapping? **one** **more than one**

Sometimes We Shared

> **Possessive pronouns** show ownership: **my**, **mine**, **your**, **yours**, **his**, **her**, **hers**, **our**, **ours**, **their**, and **theirs**.
>
> *His* house was painted red and black.

Underline the possessive pronouns in this story.

When I first saw this island, I knew it was as close to home as I could get. When the ten monks decided to join me, it became not just mine, but ours. Although we built all of these Chinese-looking buildings together, most were theirs. One hut was ours to share as a place to meditate and eat our meals. Their other buildings were used for living. One monk's hut was unusual. He had painted zebra stripes all along his walls. The monks kept their gardens around their living areas. My house was also built like the houses in China. Some of our other living quarters were more like the huts of African villages. We all lived together sharing our food and sharing what was mine, theirs, and ours.

An Archaeologist's Curse

A **possessive pronoun** shows ownership. It can replace a possessive noun. Possessive pronouns can be used before a noun or alone.

Used before: **my**, **your**, **its**, **her**, **his**, **our**, and **their**.

Used alone: **mine**, **yours**, **his**, **hers**, **yours**, and **theirs**.

Read each pair of sentences. If the correct possessive pronoun is used in the second sentence, circle **Right**. If it is not, circle **Wrong**.

1. An archaeologist studies people's remains.
   An archaeologist studies **their** remains.   Right   Wrong

2. The important discovery was the scientist's.
   The important discovery was **hers**.   Right   Wrong

3. She found part of a potter's wheel.
   She found part of **their** wheel.   Right   Wrong

4. Treasures were found on the scientist's dig.
   Treasures were found on **their** dig.   Right · Wrong

5. The pottery shards belonged to all of us.
   The pottery shards were **ours.**   Right   Wrong

6. The Pharoah's tomb took years to build.
   Their tomb took years to build.   Right   Wrong

7. The Pharoah's tomb was said to be cursed.
   Its tomb was said to be cursed.   Right   Wrong

Beware of Sharks!

A **possessive pronoun** is a pronoun that shows owner-ship. These are possessive pronouns: **my, mine, your, yours, his, her, hers, our, ours, its, their,** and **theirs.**

My car runs faster than *yours.*
Their friend went to the zoo.

Read the article. Underline each possessive pronoun.

There are many kinds of sharks, and their sizes vary greatly. They can be from 6 inches (16 cm) to over 40 feet (12 m) long. A shark doesn't have many bones in its body. Its body is quite different from yours. Much of its body is made of cartilage, which is similar to that in your nose.

Our fear of sharks is well-founded. Their behavior is unpredictable. Many a fisherman has had his catch eaten by sharks. For millions of years, the seas have been their domain, and their time on earth began long before our species appeared here.

Substitute a possessive pronoun for the words in parentheses.

1. (A shark's) _____ hearing is very sharp.

2. Sharks can hear (divers') _____ sounds under water.

3. (Dan's) _____ friend wrote a report about sharks.

4. (Janie's) _____ report gave us interesting facts.

5. The report used (Dan's and Tim's) _____ pictures.

What's Its Position?

Prepositions are words that relate nouns to other words in a sentence. They show where a noun is going, how it might be going, or to whom it might be going. Some prepositions are **in front of**, **on**, **under**, and **in**.

*I sat **in front of** my sister.*

Look at the sentences below. Underline the prepositions.

1. The tree fell behind the house.

2. I saw the movie with Sara.

3. I stepped outside the room.

4. Don't play golf in the rain.

5. I put my book next to the TV.

6. The painter climbed up the ladder.

7. We had recess inside our classroom today.

8. The driver raced around the corner.

9. The pot fell off the table.

10. The cat was hiding under the bed.

A Day on the Train

> **Prepositions** relate one word in a sentence to another by location, direction, cause, or possession. A phrase including a preposition and its modifiers is called a **prepositional phrase**.
>
> I walked **beside the road**.

Circle each preposition in the sentences below. Then underline the rest of the phrase.

1. I boarded the train at the whistle's blow.

2. I sat down by a woman in a purple dress and hat.

3. Just as I sat down, the conductor asked for my ticket.

4. We had to go to the club car for lunch.

5. For lunch we had tomato soup, potato salad, and ham sandwiches.

6. After lunch, the conductor said, "Two hours to Littleville."

7. "I think I'll take a short nap," said the woman in the purple dress.

8. My seat was by the window.

9. I spent the rest of the trip watching the world go by.

10. At three in the afternoon, we arrived in Littleville.

Two Words in One

> A **contraction** is a word made by joining two words. One or more letters are left out and an **apostrophe** replaces them.
>
> can + not = can't

Add an apostrophe to the following contractions and write the word in the blanks.

1. Im _____

2. hasnt _____

3. arent _____

4. shes _____

5. well _____

6. Ill _____

7. were _____

8. youre _____

9. thats _____

10. wed _____

Write the two words that form each of the following contractions.

1. weren't _____

2. I've _____

3. I'll _____

4. wouldn't _____

5. they're _____

6. it's _____

7. shouldn't _____

8. you'll _____

9. wasn't _____

10. you've _____

You're, Won't

A **contraction** is made by joining two words. One or more letters are left out, and an **apostrophe** replaces them.

I + will = I'll

Write the contraction for each pair of words.

1. you are _____
2. has not _____
3. we have _____
4. you had _____
5. I had _____
6. she is _____
7. they are _____
8. she would _____
9. should not _____
10. they have _____

11. they will _____
12. does not _____
13. I am _____
14. he is _____
15. will not _____
16. do not _____
17. I have _____
18. you would _____
19. cannot _____
20. we are _____

Rewrite the sentences, replacing the words in bold with the correct contraction.

1. I **do not** know if **I will** be at school tomorrow.

_____

2. If I **cannot** go, Raul said **he would** pick up my homework.

_____

A Tour of the Island

Contractions are made by putting together two words. An **apostrophe** is used in place of any letters that are left out.

we + will = we'll   *I + would = I'd*

Write the correct contraction on the line to replace the two bold words.

1. **We would** _____ take the trails up and down the hill.

2. At the top, **we will** _____ stop to look at the view.

3. Do you see the buildings? **You would** _____ see houses like those in China.

4. I **was not** _____ the only person to build this island.

5. You **would have** _____ seen monks here two years ago.

6. Since you **were not** _____ here then, **I will** _____ tell you about them.

7. **They had** _____ built great houses and gardens.

8. **They have** _____ left their mark here.

The Toon Town Diner

Homophones are words that sound the same but are spelled differently and have different meanings.

He **read** the newspaper before dinner.
His new shirt was **red** and blue.

The Toon Town Diner menu is a little confusing. Fix the homophones and write the correct words on the line after each item.

Starters

Flower Tortilla with Cheddar Cheese _____

Serial with Bananas _____

Jumbo Pretzels with Course See Salt _____

Beat Soup _____

Main Dishes

Stu with Fresh Carats _____

Stake with Son-Ripened Tomatoes _____

Ant Betsy's Country Dumplings _____

Would-Fired Pizza _____

Today's Desserts

Flaming Pairs _____

Peace of Chocolate Cake _____

Blew-berry Pie _____

Let It Snow!

Homophones are words that sound the same as other words but have different spellings and meanings. Sometimes pronouns and contractions that sound the same are confusing.

These are contractions: **it's, they're, you're, who's.**
These are possessive pronouns: **its, their, your, whose.**

It's a beautiful day!
Its beauty comes from the bright sunshine.

Circle the correct word in the parentheses for each of the following sentences.

1. (Its, It's) beginning to snow.

2. (Whose, Who's) going sledding with me?

3. Is (your, you're) new sled in the garage?

4. Hurry up, (its it's) going to be dark outside by the time (your, you're) ready.

5. Grab (your, you're) gloves and let's go!

6. We have got to find the sleds. (They're, Their) probably hanging in Grandpa's barn.

7. (Whose, Who's) that sledding down the hill?

8. It looks like David and Megan and (their, they're) little brother.

Beautiful Butterflies

commas with direct address and introductory words

Use **commas** to set apart the name of someone being addressed as well as introductory words, such as **yes**, **no**, and **well**.

Yes, they are very graceful and colorful.
*I agree with you, **Jamal**, that we need more butterflies here.*

Add commas where they belong in the following sentences.

1. Monica have you seen any butterflies fluttering around your yard?

2. Well yesterday I saw one but just for a second.

3. Betsy when was the last time you saw butterflies in your garden?

4. Two days ago Kate I saw one drinking nectar from apricot blossoms.

5. Meredith can you name the four stages of the butterfly?

6. Yes I certainly can. They are the egg, larva, chrysalis, and adult butterfly.

7. Jeff do you know the name of the butterfly's long feeding tube?

8. Yes it is called the proboscis. The butterfly uses it to drink nectar from flowers.

9. Heather did you know that the Queen Alexandra's birdwing butterfly is the largest butterfly in the world?

10. No I didn't know that.

Hip-Hop Volcano Stops

commas in a series

> **Commas** are used to separate words in a list or series.
>
> *We will need to take a train, a helicopter, a bus, and a boat to get to the island.*

This article has some punctuation problems. Help fix them by putting in commas when you see a list or series of nouns.

Sunday, May 16

We are on an expedition to visit these volcanoes: Mount Saint Helens Mount Etna Mount Pinatubo Mount Pelée and Mount Vesuvius. The members of our team are geologists botanists and volcanologists. They will help us study these volcanoes and to learn more about their formation the craters the type of volcanoes the types of eruptions and the environmental impact. There are three types of volcanoes: shield cinder cone and composite. Violent explosions or blasts from the volcano can produce lava rock fragments and gas. We will also look at the natural resources these volcanoes provide. The energy from volcanoes is used to heat homes in Iceland and to heat greenhouses growing vegetables and fruits. Geothermal steam produces electricity in Italy New Zealand the United States and Mexico.

To Aunt Betty

A **comma** is used in the greeting and closing of a letter. Commas are also used between the day, the date, and the year of a date. They also separate a city from its state.

in greeting or closing: Dear Grandma,
in date: Friday, October 27, 2000
in address: Tempe, Arizona

Jenny and Aunt Betty wrote letters to each other but forgot the commas. Fix each letter.

Sunday August 22 1999

Aunt Betty
The Little White House
Littleville California

Dear Auntie

I am so excited to come and visit you. Did you get your Model T fixed yet? Remember how it scared everyone at the Fourth of July parade? I will see you in two weeks.

Love
Jenny

Wednesday August 25 1999

Niece Jennifer
Big Brown Cottage
Bear Town Washington

Dear Jenny

I am also excited about your visit. Yes, my old clunker is fixed. We can drive to town to see my sisters. See you soon!

Love
Aunt Betty

He Said, She Said

> Use **quotation marks** to enclose the exact words of a speaker. The speaker's first word begins with a capital letter.
>
> *Mom said, "You must clean your room."*

Punctuate the following sentences correctly.

1. Dad asked John, will you be home for dinner

2. No. I will be at football practice said John

3. When will you have time to eat asked Dad

4. I'll have to eat after practice grumbled John

5. Hurry up yelled Pete

6. Pete said We'll be late for practice if you don't move faster

Punctuate and capitalize these sentences correctly.

1. will you take out the garbage today asked mom

2. mary answered i don't have time now

3. is it all right if i do it later she added

4. please do that job as soon as you get home mom said

5. Mary asked Mom will you please iron a shirt for me

Helping Out

> Use a **period** after an **abbreviation**.
> *Monday = Mon.*
> *December = Dec.*
>
> Do not use abbreviations in sentences.
> *I like to skate on Mondays in December.*

Write the correct abbreviation from the box next to each word.

Abbreviations

Blvd.	St.	Jan.	Sat.
Wed.	Feb.	P.O.	R.R.
Rd.	Apr.	Ave.	Thurs.

1. Wednesday _Wed._

2. January _Jan._

3. Street _St._

4. Boulevard _Rd_

5. February _Feb._

6. Saturday _Sat._

7. Rural Route _R.R._

8. Thursday _Thurs._

9. Avenue _Ave._

10. Road _____

11. April _Apr._

12. Post Office _P.O._

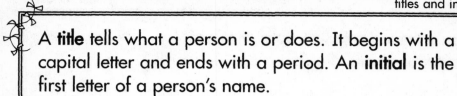

What's Your Title?

A **title** tells what a person is or does. It begins with a capital letter and ends with a period. An **initial** is the first letter of a person's name.

Mr. Rogers   *Dr. B. J. Honeycut*

Write each name and title correctly.

1. dr seuss _____

2. gen g patton _____

3. mr rogers _____

4. mrs e roosevelt _____

5. miss gloria steinem _____

6. capt james t kirk _____

7. mr m twain _____

8. dr s freud _____

9. miss louisa m alcott _____

10. mr maurice sendak _____

11. dr l pasteur _____

12. gen e braddock _____

Snow Everywhere

> Use only one **negative word** in a sentence. **Not**, **no**, **never**, and **none** are some negative words.
>
> *incorrect:* **No one nowhere** was sad when it started to snow.
>
> *correct:* **No one anywhere** was sad when it started to snow.

Circle the word in parentheses that makes the sentence correct.

1. There wasn't (no, any) snow on our grass this morning.

2. I couldn't find (no one, anyone) who wanted to build a snowman.

3. Nobody (never, ever) thinks of bringing hot cocoa.

4. We shouldn't ask (anyone, no one) to go ice skating with us.

5. None of the students could think of (nothing, anything) to do at recess except play in the new-fallen snow.

6. No one (never, ever) thinks it is a waste of time to go skating on the pond.

Write the correct word on each line that replaces the negative word in parentheses.

1. You shouldn't (never) _____ play catch with a snowball unless you want to be covered in snow.

2. Isn't (no one) _____ else going to eat icicles?

3. There wasn't (nothing) _____ wrong with using fresh snow to make our fruit drinks.

Answer Key

Page 4
1. <u>Europe</u> *contains many countries.*
2. <u>Many people in Germany</u> *work in factories.*
3. <u>France</u> *produces many different cheeses.*
4. <u>Delicious chocolates</u> *are made in Switzerland.*
5. <u>Italy</u> *is famous for its pasta.*
6. <u>Russian ballet dancers</u> *are skillful.*
7. <u>Tulips</u> *are exported from the Netherlands.*
8. <u>The British</u> *like to drink tea.*
9. <u>Norwegians</u> *like to ski.*
10. <u>Many Spaniards</u> *enjoy attending bullfights.*

Page 5
1. <u>We all</u> *climbed aboard the boat for the trip to the island.*
2. <u>Aunt Betty</u> *took the tiller, and* <u>her sisters</u> *manned the sails.*
3. <u>The wind</u> *started to pick up as we pushed off from shore.*
4. <u>The lake</u> *was very quiet.*
5. <u>A few ducks</u> *followed our boat as we left.*
6. <u>I</u> *fed them crusts of bread from our sandwiches.*
7. *As we got closer to the island,* <u>I</u> *became more and more excited.*
8. <u>Aunt Betty</u> *gave me some binoculars to try to see the island.*
9. *Just as we got near the dock,* <u>I</u> *saw a man with a long beard wearing a strange dress.*
10. *Then* <u>I</u> *saw his house, which looked like a Chinese temple.*

Page 6
1. <u>The yellow submarine</u> *submerged under the ocean.*
2. <u>The captain</u> *yelled to the crew.*
3. <u>The navigator</u> *guided the sub to its first position.*
4. *On the way,* <u>they</u> *saw beautiful fish with bright colors.*
5. <u>The crew</u> *kept close watch once the sub arrived in the bay.*
6. <u>Crew members</u> *used binoculars to survey the land.*
7. <u>The killer whales</u> *had not appeared after four hours.*
8. <u>The captain</u> *decided to dock the submarine and wait until morning.*

Page 7
1. *The killer* <u>whale</u> *is found in all oceans.*
2. *Killer* <u>whales</u>, *or orcas, travel in groups, or pods.*
3. <u>Pods</u> *can have from two to dozens of whales.*
4. *Each* <u>pod</u> *"talks" with its own set of underwater sounds.*
5. *Most of the crew* <u>members</u> *had seen orcas before.*
6. *The killer* <u>whale</u> *has teeth, unlike some other whales.*
7. *These* <u>whales</u> *feed on salmon and other fish.*
8. <u>They</u> *do not usually attack people.*

Page 8
1. *The crew* <u>decided</u> *to leave the ship and explore the ocean.*
2. *Some of the crew* <u>used</u> *snorkeling gear to explore near the surface of the water.*
3. *Others* <u>put</u> *on oxygen tanks so they could explore deeper under the water.*
4. *Each group* <u>had</u> *an hour to explore.*
5. *The snorkeling group* <u>had seen</u> *over 50 different kinds of fish by the time they returned to the sub.*
6. *The group with the oxygen tanks* <u>brought</u> *up something unusual with them.*
7. *The object* <u>was covered</u> *with barnacles and seaweed.*
8. *It* <u>was</u> *about the size of a suitcase.*

Answer Key

Page 9

1. NO	6. NO
2. CS	7. NO
3. NO	8. CS
4. CS	9. NO
5. NO	10. CS

Page 10

1. CP	6. CP
2. CP	7. NO
3. NO	8. NO
4. CP	9. NO
5. CP	10. NO

Page 11

1. Mayor Sneak called the meeting to order.
2. The escape of the circus animals was first on the agenda.
3. Mrs. Greenshoes spoke about the escape.
4. An officer suggested that all animals should be in cages.
5. All the members of the council agreed with Officer Bark.
6. The secretary wrote a letter to the Gambezi Brothers.

Page 12

1. Lanky Hank is as tall as the elephants, but Stubby Sybill is as short as her miniature pony.
2. Princess Priscilla always wears a party hat, and Prince Paulo wears a beanie.
3. Fire Hydrant Hank rides a tiny fire engine, and his dalmation rides with him.

Page 13

1. S
2. F
3. F
4. S
5. S

a., j.
b., f.
c., g.
d., h.
e., i.

Page 14

I; ?
D; .
D; .
I; ?
D; .
I; ?
D; .
D; .
D; .
I; ?
D; .
D; .

Page 15

1. "Tell me what kind of critters you see, Mrs. Greenshoes."
2. "They have big teeth! I'm scared!"*
3. "Close your windows and doors."
4. "Oh, no! They're on my porch!"*
5. "Lock your door, Mrs. Greenshoes. Officer Leash is on his way."
6. "I locked the door. I need help fast!"*
7. "Officer Leash's white truck should be there any minute. Wave to him so he knows where you are."
8. "Okay. The beast just ate my petunias!"*

Page 16

The Grand Canyon has many trails. These trails were made by deer, sheep, and the native people of the region. When the sun sets, the canyon changes color. How many colors can you see? It is very scary to look over the edge. The view is beautiful.

On the canyon wall, we saw some Native-American paintings. The designs on the rocks are called pictographs. They are symbols of objects from long ago. Have you ever seen pictographs?

We saw people running the river. Do you know what running the river is? Climb aboard! It's a chance to ride the Colorado River on a raft. Wow! You'll get the ride of your life.

Page 17
1. D; .
2. D; .
3. IN; ?
4. D; .
5. E or IM; ! or .
6. IM; .
7. E; !
8. IM; .

Page 18
1. Did the crew take underwater pictures of fish?
2. Did some fish glow in the dark like neon?
3. Did other fish glide through the water like birds through the air?
4. Did any of the crew members know the names of the fish they found?
5. Did anyone find a book in the ship's library that described most of the fish they had seen?

Page 19
Answers will vary.

Page 20
1. crowd; was
2. army; wears
3. troop; throws
4. team; marches
5. group; is
6. committee; rides
7. public; follows
8. school; has
9. choir; sings

Page 21
1. Mr. Green's, Elton Elementary
2. June, Tanya, Becky, Georgia
3. Atlanta, Fulton County Stadium
4. Tremel, Universal Studios, Orlando, Florida
5. Kennedy Space Center
6. Carla, Powell Street, San Francisco
7. Alcatraz, Golden Gate Bridge
8. Thursday, Carmen, Niagara Falls
9. Royal Gorge, Colorado

Page 22
Point Imperial, Grand Canyon, Phantom Ranch, Kaibab Trail, Colorado River, Arizona, Native American, Havasu Canyon, Rampart Cave

Page 23
Singular Nouns:
1. girl, field
3. bunny, bush
Plural Nouns:
1. deer
2. Squirrels, sides, trees
4. children, Canada geese
5. Pictures, books, children, animals

Sentences will vary.

Page 24
mothers, fathers, benches, games, teams, cheers, hits, strikes, catches, teammates, coaches, kids

Page 25
1. babies
2. turkeys
3. knives
4. skies
5. pansies
6. guppies
7. elves
8. wives
9. tries
10. keys
11. boys
12. shelves
13. ladies
14. chimneys
15. hooves
16. gypsies
17. monkeys
18. lobbies

Answer Key

Page 26
1. tortillas
2. peaches
3. boxes
4. candies
5. girls
6. men
7. families
8. leaves
9. beans

Page 27
1. her
2. him
3. her
4. it
5. it
6. us
7. it

Page 28
1. it, they, them
2. it, they
3. they, it, he
4. It, they, it
5. He, it
6. them
7. them, it

Page 29
1. We
2. me
3. I
4. us
5. me
6. I

Page 30
penguins, air, air sacs, penguins, water, nest, eggs, male, eggs, eggs, skin flap, babies, babies, babies

Page 31
1. V
2. N
3. N
4. V
5. N
6. V
7. N
8. V
9. N
10. V

Page 32
1. walk, run
2. throw
3. drop, throw
4. hike, camp
5. Build
6. Store
7. Stop, pass
8. take, wear

Page 33
1. Yes
2. No
3. No
4. Yes
5. No
6. No
7. Yes
8. No
9. Yes
10. Yes

Page 34
1. were
2. had, was
3. is
4. were, went

Page 35
1. chases
2. won
3. wears
4. delivered
5. sang
6. raced
7. opens
8. tied
9. worked

Page 36
1. studied
2. baked
3. smelled
4. washed
5. smiled
6. grabbed
7. copied
8. trimmed
9. named
10. spied
11. melted
12. clipped
13. toasted
14. popped
15. emptied
16. played

Page 37
1. sang
2. ran
3. went, bought
4. found, rode
5. put, swam
6. flew, found
7. went, found
8. found, ate

Page 38
1. fell
2. took
3. ran
4. broke
5. knew
6. began
7. threw
8. ate
9. slept

Page 39
Chart: did, gone, knew, fell, spoken, stood, wrote, drawn

1. went
5. heard

2. fallen
3. stood
4. ran

6. sat
7. took

9. <u>has</u> given
10. <u>have</u> seen

Page 40
1. This afternoon I will pick up groceries at the store.
2. I will call the painter to paint the shutters.
3. The neighborhood will build a float for the parade next Friday.
4. The picnic lunch at City Hall will be tomorrow.
5. Jenny will come on Thursday.

Page 41
Answers will vary.
2. might listen
3. did eat

4. will do
5. are going

Page 42
Main:
1. seen
2. tell
3. working
4. gone
5. swimming
6. chew

7. get
8. marry
9. been
10. finish
11. been

Helping:
1. Have
2. did
3. am
4. has
5. is
6. should

7. cannot
8. Did
9. have
10. might
11. have

Page 43
1. <u>has</u> come
2. <u>have</u> written
3. <u>have</u> wondered
4. <u>have</u> waited
5. <u>have</u> learned
6. <u>have</u> planned
7. <u>have</u> made
8. <u>have</u> known

Page 44
1. is, was
2. are, were
3. are, were

4. am, was
5. is
6. is

Page 45
1. is
2. is
3. am
4. was
5. were

6. was
7. is
8. was
9. was
10. are

Page 46
1. helping, been
2. helping, was
3. main, were
4. helping, was
5. main, is

1. has been
2. will be
3. will be

Page 47
1. did
2. done
3. does
4. do
5. does

6. does
7. don't
8. doesn't
9. did
10. does

Page 48
1. Those, lovely, pink, five
2. These, white, a, sweet
3. Each, several, dainty
4. The, refreshing, the, sweet-scented, the
5. These, five, colorful, tall

Which one?: Those, These, a, Each, The, the, the, These
What kind?: lovely, pink, white, sweet, dainty, refreshing, sweet-scented, colorful, tall

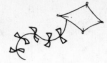

Answer Key

How many?: five, several, five

Page 49
1. coldest
2. warmest
3. hotter
4. deepest
5. deeper
6. windiest
7. strongest
8. foggiest
9. rainiest

Page 50
Answers may vary slightly.
   The, An, A, the, the, The, the, a, A, the, an, a, The, the, a, the, the, an

---

Page 51
- carefully, up, quickly, Tragically
- quietly, slowly, still, quietly, slowly

Page 52
1. always
2. near
3. far
4. generously
5. frequently
6. slowly, carefully
7. cautiously

Page 53
1. higher, highest   2. faster, fastest

1. more/less   4. most/least
2. most/least   5. more/less
3. more/less

Page 54
1. good   5. real
2. well   6. well
3. really   7. well
4. really   8. surely

Page 55
1. one   5. more than one
2. more than one   6. more than one
3. one   7. one
4. one

Page 56
mine, ours, theirs, ours, our, Their, his, their, their, My, our, our, mine, theirs, ours

---

Page 57
1. Right   5. Right
2. Right   6. Wrong
3. Wrong   7. Wrong
4. Wrong

Page 58
their, its, Its, yours, its, your, Our, Their, his, their, their, our

1. Its   4. Her
2. their   5. their
3. His

Page 59
1. behind   6. up
2. with   7. inside
3. outside   8. around
4. in   9. off
5. next to   10. under

Page 60
1. at the whistle's blow
2. by a woman; in a purple dress and hat
3. for my ticket
4. to the club; for lunch
5. For lunch
6. After lunch; to Littleville
7. in the purple dress
8. by the window
9. of the trip
10. At three; in the afternoon; in Littleville

Answer Key

Page 61

1. I'm
2. hasn't
3. aren't
4. she's
5. we'll

6. I'll
7. we're
8. you're
9. that's
10. we'd

1. were not
2. I have
3. I will
4. would not
5. they are

6. it is
7. should not
8. you will
9. was not
10. you have

Page 62

1. you're
2. hasn't
3. we've
4. you'd
5. I'd
6. she's
7. they're
8. she'd
9. shouldn't
10. they've

11. they'll
12. doesn't
13. I'm
14. he's
15. won't
16. don't
17. I've
18. you'd
19. can't
20. we're

1. I don't know if I'll be at school tomorrow.
2. If I can't go, Raul said he'd pick up my homework.

Page 63

1. We'd
2. we'll
3. You'd
4. wasn't
5. would've
6. weren't, I'll
7. They'd
8. They've

Page 64

flour
cereal
coarse, sea
beet
stew, carrots
steak, sun
aunt
wood
pears
piece
blue

Page 65

1. It's
2. Who's
3. your
4. it's, you're
5. your
6. They're
7. Who's
8. their

Page 66

1. Monica,
2. Well,
3. Betsy,
4. Two days ago, Kate,
5. Meredith,
6. Yes,
7. Jeff,
8. Yes,
9. Heather,
10. No,

Page 67

- Mount Saint Helens, Mount Etna, Mount Pinatubo, Mount Pelée, and Mount Vesuvius.
- geologists, botanists, and volcanologists.
- their formation, the craters, the type of volcanoes, the types of eruptions, and the environmental impact.
- shield, cinder cone, and composite.
- lava, rock fragments, and gas.
- Italy, New Zealand, the United States, and Mexico.

Answer Key

Page 68

Sunday, August 22, 1999
Littleville, California
Dear Auntie,
Love,

Wednesday, August 25, 1999
Bear Town, Washington
Dear Jenny,
Love,

3. Mr. Rogers
4. Mrs. E. Roosevelt
5. Miss Gloria Steinem
6. Capt. James T. Kirk
7. Mr. M. Twain
8. Dr. S. Freud
9. Miss Louisa M. Alcott
10. Mr. Maurice Sendak
11. Dr. L. Pasteur
12. Gen. E. Braddock

Page 69

1. Dad asked, "John, will you be home for dinner?"
2. "No. I will be at football practice," said John.
3. "When will you have time to eat?" asked Dad.
4. "I'll have to eat after practice," grumbled John.
5. "Hurry up!" yelled Pete.
6. Pete said, "We'll be late for practice if you don't move faster."

1. "Will you take out the garbage today?" asked Mom.
2. Mary answered, "I don't have time now."
3. "Is it all right if I do it later?" she added.
4. "Please do that job as soon as you get home," Mom said.
5. Mary asked, "Mom, will you please iron a shirt for me?"

Page 70

1. Wed.
2. Jan.
3. St.
4. Blvd.
5. Feb.
6. Sat.
7. R.R.
8. Thurs.
9. Ave.
10. Rd.
11. Apr.
12. P.O.

Page 71

1. Dr. Seuss
2. Gen. G. Patton

Page 72

1. any
2. anyone
3. ever
4. anyone
5. anything
6. ever

1. ever
2. anyone
3. anything